"Do not miss Me in your striving;
I am not looking for perfection.
I do not see you as broken.
My Grace is always with you."

Acknowledgments

Thank You, Lord, for writing with me, writing to me and encouraging my heart to be my equilibrium. Though I may fall to find myself living in my head at times, You always call me back Home. Thank You for helping me to clean out the clutter of collected wounds through our emotional exchanges. Thank You for acknowledging my love and embracing me so Intimately. I only ask You help me to share this Love with others — that they, too, can find rest in themselves with You at Home in their hearts; where You can find rest as they carry You.

Thank you, Mom and Dad, for always providing a home — a heart of unconditional love, understanding and freedom to process; a sacred writing space — a sanctuary where my soul could grow ever more intimate with Jesus — and for compassionately respecting the simultaneous power and delicacy of the Mystical experience.

Thank you, Sam, for so much patience, encouragement, understanding and dedication. Thank you for being so careful and attentive to detail — for we both know these seeds do not germinate in me. Thank you for your willingness to walk through your fears and take on tasks you doubted were within your capacity. Thank you for opening up to your heart, for always treating with great respect the dignity of how sacred to my heart is this experience with Mystery. And so importantly, thank you for your willingness to walk through your own friendship with Mystery.

Thank you, Mike Precopio, for your encouragement, insight and support in bringing fourth the revelations and contemplations on these pages.

Thank you, Fran and Dolores, for all these years of encouragement and support; for listening and sharing; for respect and truth.

Thank you, George, for your wonderful gift of knowing exactly when I would be in need of a new journal — a new pillow — and a phone call or letter. Thank you for the gift of your genuine and gentle spirit.

Thank you, Chrissy, G.J. and Rick, for reminding me — exactly when needed — who I am.

Thank you, Veronica, for the consistent, "right on," timely prayers. Thank you, Carl Lohmann, proprietor of Carl Grove studios, for your generous spirit and technical support.

Thank you, all who continue to seek to understand and appreciate the dignity of the soul for the sake of compassion, purity of heart and healing.

To all who have ever lifted me in prayer for all these years, I can't even begin...

...and Drink the Liquid Sound of Wisdom...

Resting in the Womb of God

second edition

Contents

...and Drink the Liquid Sound of Wisdom...

Resting in the Womb of God

second edition

© 2025 Kimberlyann DeAngelo / Samuel Zimmerman
All rights reserved.

Published by Kimberlyann DeAngelo / Samuel Zimmerman
for One Heart Love.

Book typeset & design by Carl Grove Studios

ISBN 979-8-218-86189-6

oneheartlove.com

Introduction

Kimberlyann DeAngelo was born Kimberlyann Storz on January 8th, 1966, in Jefferson Hospital, PA., the second of two daughters to Alfred and Mary Storz. From the beginning of her life, unique health issues remained undiagnosed until she was in her thirties. Eventually, she was diagnosed with a condition known as Undefined Connective Tissue Disease, an autoimmune disorder that manifests itself in symptoms of other diseases. She also suffered from a digestive disease, a collapsed artery pressing on her duodenum and small intestines that caused lack of proper blood flow.

At four years of age, she was taken to her doctor's office where an emergency procedure using a scope was performed. In the process of trying and failing to find a congenital defect, they believed they accidentally ruptured her colon. She was rushed to Haverford Community Hospital which did not ordinarily treat children but made an exception in her extreme case. Her parents were faced with a monumental decision; should they give permission to perform surgery on someone so young and fragile that it could result in her death? Yet, if her colon was actually ruptured and they did nothing, toxins from it could seep into her body, making her death imminent. A hurried, prayerful, life-or-death decision to operate was made.

Kim endured critical events which defined her physical and spiritual journey. During surgery, she had her first of multiple near-death experiences when she was briefly lost as she flat-lined. She recalls a sense of warmth, peace, bright light, and an undefinable familiarity of knowing where she was going. Kim has never been able to accurately describe the pure encounter of being with God but maintains that when we are infants and children, we are closer to that "naked and unmasked beginning;" the memory of perfect Love that fades as we grow up in a world where endless distractions, conflicts, and ever-increasing complexities have drawn us away from the knowledge of our oneness with each other and our Source.

As an adult, Kim would eventually speak with a therapist who worked with people who also had near-death experiences. After relaying her history to him, including the fact that during the surgery, as she came back from the "Light, A fire that lit me aflame, but did not burn me," she felt it was God rejecting her and she felt unworthy of the many blessings in her own life. Her therapist asked her to consider that maybe it was God saying, "There's more for you to do." Just before finding her therapist, she relived her first neardeath experience in dreams on two consecutive nights.

Throughout Kim's life, she could see the pain that ran far below the surface in family, friends, and strangers alike. She would have the uncontrollable sense of wanting to comfort and cheer them up, as other's grief, physical pain and suffering would move through her as if it were her own.

Kim's experiences, however, weren't limited to the living. Since childhood, she could sense the spirits of the departed. Her bedroom walls were lined with stuffed animals like a barrier and she would go to sleep with music as a shield against forces she couldn't understand. Present too was a deep devotion to God, praying often with an intuitive understanding of a Higher Power and the belief she would one day become a nun. Years later, she appealed to an Order but was declined because of her "health issues." Kim learned from her father early in life to "see God in others" and that "God is within."

Growing up, she was a tomboy, thin and fair-skinned with a pixie haircut. Her wild, red hair led to being teased by many. She enjoyed climbing trees, playing dodge ball, and "kick the can" in the streets of her Philadelphia home.

During her 8th grade year at Haverford Jr. High, 14-year-old Kim had just finished studying at the school's library and was crossing the school parking lot when a gang of about ten boys who had just finished football practice (some of whom she knew as friends) grabbed her and dragged her into the boys' bathroom. It was after school hours so no one could hear her yelling and screaming as she fought them trying to tear off her cloths and rape her. She managed to escape. Sadly, at her

17th surprise birthday party, this nightmare was repeated at her friend's home when a drunken boy she did not know raped her. Reflecting on this, Kim recalled:

At first, there's the shock. For some reason, many women go through this feeling of guilt; it must be something they did, something they brought on. They are made to feel it is their fault. What helped me get beyond all that was not only feeling my own sadness and pain but also truly feeling sorry for them. I felt a lot of pain for them because for having done what they did says to me that they were lacking love from somewhere, whether it was from their family, their parents, or somewhere else. Something inside of them had to be hurting to be able to do that to someone else. I was feeling my hurt and theirs too.

Much of the events surrounding the incident were suppressed for almost seven years. Kim discovered later that 5 to 7 years is the average amount of time before victims begin to remember little bits and pieces of such horrific events.

To say "victim"
gives you power
over me
a survivor
doesn't it
But "survivor"
one of your
survivors adds
another notch
doesn't it
puts you on a
pedestal
as if I'm thanking
you
for making me
"great" "strong"
a "survivor"
again
giving you
power
Until I see feel
no more of you
Until you can't
make me (run)

Until you don't I
own
the memory where
you are nothing
but coward
and I am
neither "victim"
nor "survivor" I
just am I
am just
dreaming...

When this is your story
it is not your story
it is part of
who you are
It is the salt
you can't taste
in tears that chisel
chisel
chisel your heart
numb to the pain
until you see
your name

again and again
every time you hear
another's cry
see another's stare
from wounded eyes
until you see
your name again
and again
every time you hear
"rape"

KimberlyannDeAngelo
"Not My Story"
3/4/01

One thing that helped her recovery was to stop beating herself up for not being able to move on and just get over it. "I was getting over it. I was moving on. I was opening myself to relationships. I participated in a study for Women Organized Against Rape. I spoke out and did poetry readings for benefits about it. I went to schools and spoke about it.

But it's part of me; it's still part of me. It happens to women of all ages and all cultures. It has happened throughout history in many different ways. But, one of these days, the dignity of women's souls and women's hearts are going to be fully respected. I have faith in this."

It was her closest girlfriend's birthday and Kim was repeatedly asked to attend. By now, she had distanced herself from the party scene; working, writing, and living a simple and quiet life. She went out for dinner with her parents that evening, and her mother asked if she really wanted to go to her friend's party (ordinarily, her mother encouraged her socialization). But Kim was insistent on being there for her friend.

At 17, she had not yet obtained a driver's license so that night, an old Camaro pulled up to her Havertown, PA residence. Kim and her four friends headed to Westchester. Her friends had already been drinking. They partied for hours and it was early morning by the time they were ready to leave. Unfortunately, the friend who had driven everyone had passed out. It was too late, Kim thought, to call her father for a ride so she decided to let her friend sleep it off. At about 4:00 am, all five finally headed home with Kim in the front passenger seat. Most often, she would turn the radio on and roll down the window but, this time, she just sat back.

They found themselves on a winding road and in unfamiliar territory. Suddenly, the car struck a tree, throwing it up on its nose and tumbling down an embankment. Kim felt the sensation of being outside of her body. She could see herself in the car, witnessing the accident. She could see the driver being thrown out of his door. She could see her friend, who was sitting in the middle of the back seat, being thrown through the windshield and she could see the others, still in the car, but unconscious. The entire front of the Camaro was caved in except for a box around her. Suddenly, she found herself back in her body. Something had punctured her right shin and metal from the rear view mirror cut the top of her head. Shards of broken glass pierced her body from her neck down but her face was left unharmed. Finding her door jammed, she crawled through the open driver's side door and looked at the others. She could not tell if they were alive but quickly sought help.

Kim soon came to the home of two older women who looked out a window in response to her knocking. Seeing blood on her face, they panicked and stayed inside. She finally turned to see a man smoking a cigarette near some bushes. This image triggered unsettling memories. Fearing she might get raped again, Kim collapsed in front of the house. The man must have realized she was injured and frightened so he got his wife to call 911.

Following the accident, the police took Kim's parents to see the totaled car. One of the officers who was on the force for 28 years told them he had never seen anything like it and that no one should have survived, even though everyone did survive; not withstanding the fact two of her friends had to spend a considerable amount of time in recovery.

In her early 20s, Kim was admitted to Paoli Hospital. One of the things she was being tested for was leukemia. And because of her continuous weight loss, she was put on a feeding pump which she decorated and named Harry. He became her "dancing partner" and she would walk with him down the halls. She shared a room with an elderly nun named Sister Joan, who showed great kindness to her and her mother. A former missionary nun, now in her 80s, who had never been sick a day in her life, suddenly blacked out while attending church and was rushed to the emergency room. They hooked her up to a feeding pump just like Kim's. On one of Kim's walks, she was returning to her room and saw Sister Joan nodding off in her chair. Kim's heart went out to her because she seemed alone. Walking up to her, she gently asked, "Sister Joan, won't you come for a walk with Harry and me?" At first, Sister Joan looked at her in puzzlement but a big smile quickly beamed across her face. Kim took her hand and they began their first of many walks down the halls together. When it came time for Sister Joan to be discharged, she gave Kim and her mother a St. Jude medal (patron saint of hope and impossible causes) blessed at Lourdes, France and acquired on one of her many overseas missions.

At one point, during Kim's hospitalization, her doctor decided to do a bone marrow biopsy on her hip. He told her this was usually an outpatient procedure and relatively safe, requiring only a local anesthetic. A few hours after the biopsy, however, Kim started to hemorrhage severely. She was placed flat on her stomach so they could stack twenty-five pound sandbags over the wound in a desperate effort to stop the bleeding. After three days of such severe hemorrhaging, Kim needed blood and platelet transfusions. Then, around 9:00 one night, a nurse who was holding gauze over the wound said to Kim's mother, "I have to change this dressing. It's been bleeding way more than usual and I don't understand why it won't stop. I'm going to call the doctor. Can you please hold this gauze down and apply pressure?" Mary complied and, as she did, Kim felt a heating sensation and a sense of peace. She knew the bleeding had stopped. When the nurse returned, Mary lifted the gauze and the nurse exclaimed, "Oh my God!" Pressing around the wound, she asked Mary what she had done to make it stop bleeding. Mary opened her hands and showed her the St. Jude medal that Sister Joan had given them. She had held it to the wound and prayed silently.

By the time Kim was about 30, she had been to numerous hospitals and treatment facilities concerning her weight loss and digestive problems. There was a belief among the medical community that this was deliberate and self-induced. Weighing in at 70 pounds, she was placed in another eating disorder program where she adhered to the strict feeding regimen in place for her. She would receive a certain amount of food per tray and trays per meal, three times a day, along with a dietary supplement drink between meals. But rather than increase, her weight declined. The doctor running the facility at that time was convinced it was because of something Kim was doing. He thought she was either taking laxatives, making herself vomit, or exercising in her room to lose weight. Under this presumption, they decided to place Kim in a wheelchair in which she had to stay to keep her from doing anything that would expend even an eighth of a calorie. She was not allowed to sleep, shower, or go to the bathroom alone, and was placed on 24-

hour surveillance. Months passed and even with such severe restrictions, while still adhering to the feeding regimen, Kim continued to lose weight and grow steadily worse. The doctor and hospital became greatly concerned because the insurance company threatened to withhold paying her hospital bill over their failure to help Kim. At this point, the doctor contemplated having her court-committed to Norristown State Hospital, a mental institution.

By now, Kim wasn't speaking very much, just writing and drawing. Then, one evening, a doctor from the University of Pennsylvania Hospital came to see her. He had seen the results of her blood work and examined her case. Approaching her, he got on his knees and put one hand on her face and the other on her knee, and said, "I'm getting you out of here." He went to the head doctor and insisted on her removal, saying, "You better put her in a medical facility or you're going to have a lawsuit on your hands because you are killing her." Even though he complied and she was transferred to Presbyterian Hospital, the head doctor was still so convinced that she should be court-committed, he asked a top psychiatrist from Philadelphia to evaluate her. This expert psychiatrist spent considerable time with her and, after many sessions, took her hand and said, "That doctor wanted me to write you up to have you court-committed. He's going to be surprised when he gets my write-up be-cause there's nothing wrong with your mind. You're a woman who has not been heard all these years." Kim would later say, "They actually had me convinced at some point that it was all in my head and that my digestive problems were my own fault. I know others who had some serious illness they couldn't figure out and they were put through the mental health system to eventually learn they had a rare disease or some rare form of cancer. I don't care about the visible, physical scars on my body, but the emotional and psychological scars are far more wounding. Am I afraid of sharing my story? Yes. But if I can help someone else who's going through something similar to hang on and know they are sane, then it will be worth it... "

Every scar the many
scars
have become my body's
map
of culture on my emotions
culture on my spirit
to mark roads
taken as a soul lost
from itself
in a world of physical
that seeks only perfection
for eyes
two eyes one sided
that won't bring focus
to vision
of a third
to see on through
all around
that we are never
lost just a distance
from perfect —
perfect view
perfect sound
perfect Love
Every scar the many
to my body
imperfect
have become the map
of culture
on my emotions
my spirit
to take me back
Home.

Kimberlyann
DeAngelo
8/11/01

At this point, her marriage of 7 years had fallen apart. Kim prefers not to discuss the details of her marriage in order to protect the privacy of all parties involved. She was on home health care and even though her mother worked full time, she still supported her by helping her take care of her apartment and by staying with her whenever she was in the hospital. Soon, it became too much for her mother to handle and Kim felt awful watching those closest to her suffer through it all. With all the hospitalizations that Kim endured, no answers for the cause of her illness or the often terrifying and spiritually illuminat-ing visions, dreams, and empathic events were produced. She felt there was no one she could talk to about these experienes. On her last stay, her condition continued to deteriorate. By this time, she weighed considerably less than 70 pounds. She was discharged with a prescription for 50 mg. Demerol tablets for pain.

One Sunday afternoon around 4:00, Mary had just left and Kim knew her home health care nurse wouldn't return until 11:00 the next morning. She thought, "Plenty of time to do this." She put a favorite record on, swallowed the entire bottle of pain medicine, and relaxed on the sofa. All night, she slipped away, finally saying to God, "Thank You, Father. I'm so sorry. I'm not quitting but I can't watch everybody suffer, and I can't make You or I suffer like this anymore. I don't understand." Hands lifted her up as she convulsed and a voice spoke, saying, "No, you're not done, you're not done..." over and over. At some point, the record jammed and began repeating her Nevil Brothers' version of "Amazing Grace."

The next morning, Kim's nurse found her and called for an ambulance which took her to the hospital. Multiple EEG's were performed and found no residual effects. She was told that it was a miracle she survived and considering her weight, and the amount of Demerol taken, she should at least have had some damage to her brain or be in a coma.

She spent years searching for a spiritual counselor seeking help to try to understand these profound experiences. Finally, help came unexpectedly in the writings of two mystic saints, St. Catherine of Siena and St. Teresa of Avila. "It's like I live things or come to these understandings; messages or life experiences are given, and then I'll pick up the writings of St. Catherine again and start reading, and it's exactly what I was just going through, giving me more understanding."

Now, at this time, while she and I were each renting a room in the same house, many profound experiences occurred. One such incident was when The Blessed Mother appeared to her, resting her head ove Kim's stomach. Another extremely profound experience was when Jesus showed Himself while Kim was on her knees crying out, "Why all this suffering?" Kim was undergoing chemo therapy treatments that caused cold sores as a side effect. And as she was holding a napkin over her bleeding lip, she was suddenly showered in indescribable peace and as she pulled the napkin away and looked at it, Jesus placed His crucified image on the napkin with the blood from her lip which was suddenly healed. Shortly after, she wrote, "I give You my life as prayer."

Another time, as Kim was washing her face, the Lord showed her in the mirror His golden Light all around her and her face and body as a silhouette. She prayed to God, "You are showing me, Lord, Your Light that's with me. If there is anything You need me to hear tonight, please let me be an unobstructed vessel." That is when the writing "Darkness Switched on the Light" came to her. Recently reflecting on this work and "Rivulet Compassionate," Kim said, "Many people say I choose to suffer. But I'm coming to an understanding that it is not within my control. As I look at those prayers and those experiences, I look at my life and that cross on the napkin. It's beyond my understanding. I just know that I'm not mine."

In spite of the health issues and traumatic events Kim endured and continues to live through, she's had a rich, full life. She went to school for business and nutrition, ran a supermarket natural food section, and held management positions. While living in rural Pennsylvania, she ran her own natural food store, forming close ties with the community. She was involved in landscape architecture and studied horticulture. She worked one-on-one with Down Syndrome and autistic children, the developmentally disabled and severely handicapped. She volunteered at a senior center, teaching arts and crafts, and taught English as a second language. She ran open poetry readings at The Point in Bryn Mawr Pennsylvania and collaborated lyrically with songwriters, to list just some of her accomplishments.

She currently leads a quiet, devoted life to the Heart of Christ and the caregiving of her parents.

About the Poetry

As you read through these works, you will see a distinctive rhythm to much of the writing. Some pieces seem to "dance" across the page. The spontaneous nature of Kim's writings are a personal and vital component of her experience. I have preserved the original format of each piece, copying, as accurately as possible, from a range of journals of various sizes. Titles and dates where the author recorded them have been included. When asked why she does not title every piece, Kim replied, "Many times I don't have a title, I guess, because my life seems to be one long expression." I find this to be true in her case because of the remarkable harmony of the finished book. Even in times of extreme pain, Kim is very prolific. When it was decided that the first book would be a collection of her prayers and spiritual writings, I spent many hours sorting through her spiritual and secular works for appropriate material.

The final collection, though written many years and miles apart, yields a continuity like the peaks and valleys through a person's life. Here is Kim's most intimate dialogue with God within which there is a sense of a Divine hand in the arrangement. God's dialogue with her has been italicized and all non-standard capitalizations of words are in reference to Divinity. Duplicated as well are her created words and alternate spellings.

About the "cross on the napkin"

The image on the inside cover is the crucifix formed on the napkin previously mentioned in this introduction. The cross on the napkin was eventually put under glass for protection. It was with reluctance that Kim finally consented to make this public knowledge. It is not only an extremely personal event but the kind of thing that may invite uninformed criticism or judgment. I can only attest to the authenticity of the image and the reality of Kim's spirit. She has never desired to profit from nor create conflict over this or anything she's said, written, or experienced.

Samuel Zimmerman

2025

“the heart in the stream” photo by
Kimberlyann DeAngelo

Time in Hands
not of ours does not pass,
it grows.

†††

Some of us are given to
a life of contemplation
over things "spiritual," "philosophical,"
"metaphysical" — whatever
you wish to call it. There
are days this can be a
tremendous burden, curse
of torment; mostly it becomes
a great blessing. We may
play here and there with
"silly;" mingle a little
in "worldly;" fall into
"statistical" for a moment,
but where we truly hang
out is in the deep crevices
of our soul where our
fruit ripens to expose
color, bruises and Core.

As we ripen and expose
we fade our color to vibrant
Light as we accept our
bruises from reason that
seeks no reason or blame
—with compassion we
take the Hands that gently
or powerfully squeeze to
see how supple, pliable,
close to the Core we are.

We don't mind sitting
among the bin of "strange,"
"unusual," "alien," rough-
and-bumpy-what-truck-
did-we-just-fall-off-of
"Ugli" fruit. We find
more beauty in knowing
who we are.

Interesting... Ugli
fruits are often more
expensive, considered "exotic."
A soul covers great mileage seeking
to return from exportation
back to importation as
it learns this world's
common denominator is
not peace, beauty and
harmony, but rather
the journey of outreach
through suffering, chaos
and tragedy to unite
us that takes us there.

2/29/08

†††

Father,
You touch me, I create.
You call to me, I speak silently
in write
You teach me, I listen and sketch.
You tell me to go, I reach out
no hesitation or doubt...

As one responding to the gifts
You have given me and seriously
contemplating that responsibility,
I urge You to offer me protection
through Wisdom and discernment
— as to the creative out-
pouring under which I succumb
and how to bring it forth in
a positive light of hope, to not
present nor influence negativity.
Yet, believing so, as I do, in
the importance of processing
negative emotions and experiences
through Your muse of power
inside, I must not neglect
that piece of the creative
journey. For it is necessary
to be enlightened to and on all of our
emotional levels, including —
especially — suffering. To
know one emotion we must
know its opposite.

To grow toward our ascension we must
come to steadfast and loyal
faith through the beauty and
the murk; we must remain
open to life and all of its many
colors, joyrides, twists and trials
— knowing all the while
the Grace, compassion and encouragement
there for us to receive is also
there for us to give. We must
remain open to ways of gaining
knowledge and understanding
so as to help others along.
For it may be that in sharing
negative emotions through our
art we help another process
theirs and rid themselves of
those shadows.

We must not fear turning down
the sun
to bring about the darkness
under which we become undone
so we can see (know) our souls
more clearly in the dawn.

3/10/06

†††

Baptism
(Leave Me Clean of Me)

Sometimes I wish to find You
where I am
and dance on the magical whim
sea inside of me...

Sometimes I wish to part my bangs
lift my hair and see Your Eyes
melt my lips apart
with the tongue of Your heart...

Lay with me in green green grass
Roll me down hallowed hills
of cheeks blushing unearthed manna
in fringe-hemmed land Bohemia
Cover me under the Face of Love
raise me in the heat of Your sun
Scar me in stars to quell my fears
then cool me off
heal me in trust
to rest adorned in moon-
glow of Your Light —
Salvation, salivate
savage vibration
Christen me untamed
Leave me Christened untamed

...Fill my womb with the Wisdom
of maturity to birth Love selflessly
giving (beyond) over to You (beyond)
any need to receive...

Let me not lie down
only to rest awaiting Your hand
upon my breast where here
on the surface
may satisfy some mortal ideal...

Ignite my awareness
to recognize Your Voice, to concern
my heart with its conscience;
to concern my heart to reflect patience
where Love's Mercy lingers in balance
and calls us to return to our state
of Grace...

Gently play with me
my game of imperfections
rising from any claim
of insecurity, avarice
or vanity over me...

Leave me not a virgin
to lie awaiting virtue
to penetrate sanctification...
Raise me up
in progressive transformation
Raise us up
in progressive transformation...

Amen

2/28/06

†††

I am determined to be Love

†††

I once thought that Love
was only what was good
until I was old enough (spiritually)
to realize I was too young (spiritually)
then to understand
even the experiences of
anger, resentment, pain
and disbelief —
in what had just been done,
what had just been said,
what I had just seen —
were really Love in grief...
Though a child,
beneath those emotions
I did always respond
to the call of compassion
that without thought
wanted only to comfort
the wounded, that did
not judge those who harmed,
but wanted to extend
to them an arm.
For some reason,
I needed to suffer
alongside all —
the good, the bad,
the ugly —
for any of this
could, too, reside
in me.
I could feel the need
through all disguise
for Love,
the craving for healing
a separation
none of us could explain...

Many said, "You are naive,
too nice, too trusting."
I did not know I would
walk, crawl, collapse
in such numerous
traumatic and hurtful
experience
to crumble into
guarded-hearted-
hardness
to detour my path
in this hour,
skew the natural
rhythm of spirit to
my soul...

I wonder if, like the
rings to the grain
in the wood of a tree
that tell us how old it is,
we could count the wounds
of a heart, if we could
literally hold that heart
in our hands and feel

the weight of those wounds —
if we could remove
each bandage to see this heart
in its purity...
would this tell us
how old that soul is
to reveal blood
that runs deeper
from life upon life
gone by;
to reveal it is as
ancient as the essence
of Love?
Could we then once and
for all, <u>scientifically,</u>
<u>literally, tangibly</u>
see this essence of
Love is in <u>all</u> —
the "good" the "bad"
and "ugly"?

†††

Love unconditional, acceptance,
forgiveness...
that is my soul's truth...
And however that is to be expressed
is in accordance to another's need,
spoken to me through their physical
presence or distant energy;
spoken through a calling upon
my heart, spontaneous,
in the moment's need —
attention, acknowledgment,
freedom — through prayer,
letter, phone, silence, absence,
visit, touch, word, music,
laughter, dance, stillness
of my tongue, gratitude,
guidance from my own experience,
encouragement from perspective
outside of their own...

To walk barefoot in response
to need with soles that move more
deeply than my physical
capabilities; to love outside
of and beyond understanding,
that is what Wisdom tells me
my soul's truth is, and that
nothing else matters — where I live,
what I study, what I
have or don't have...

All that I ask in return
    is for respect of the need
    my soul has to be free
    to love freely —
    so to hear, feel and
    respond in the moment's
    callings...

To those who have given
    and do give this back
    to me, thank you for coming
    to me with your need
    and reciprocating in mine
    in ways that do not hold "neediness",
    in ways that do not approach
    treading upon nor suffocating
    the other's spirit — yours
    or mine — in ways
    that do not block Life /
    Love from its continuum...

Again, in Love, I give you
    to your truth, for, again,
    yours is mine and mine is yours,
    after all free will is
    given us even by our own
    Creator...

In freedom
there is always desire
to return

Possessiveness, ownership, attachment
only bind us
to the experience of loss
as they push desire
to turn away and run

It's a funny thing about freedom
Selfishness tells us
it can't be found in selflessness
But that is where its wings mend
That is where its wings open
That is where its wings fly.

3/24/07

†††

I ask for vision and insight
that feeds Agape Love in & from me...
I ask, Father, that I know
intuitively Your Will in the
situations and changing moments
of my life; that I have the
love and courage inside and
around me to follow that Will,
to respond positively to that Will.
I ask for vision and insight
into Your Will for others so that
I may respect their needs and
soul's desires from a Love of more
purity — a Love that encourages,
prays for them to follow that call
as I let go of selfish "needs" that may
stem from attachment or any
surface superficiality, any intellectual
or cerebral opinion that believes
"I know best."
I ask for a heart continuously
filled with a love of charity for others and the
humility to ask when I need; to gratefully
receive while believing I am worthy of receiving.
I ask that even in the
tumultuous turns and, sometimes,
wrecks life can present that I
find peace in knowing I was, am,
following Your Will.

I ask to be a place of peaceful
rest and mercy for others, for You.
I ask, if it be Your Will, that
I may be a channel for Your Vision
for others — that my thoughts, actions,
words, my sensuality, my body may
sing in the "Liquid Sound of Wisdom."

Again, Father,

breathe Wisdom in me
to birth Wisdom through me...

2/26/07

†††

Did I listen today…
to myself
to God
to anyone?

Did I walk through today…
suffering with
myself
God
anyone?

Did I love today…
myself no so
God yes no
anyone? yes

Did I encourage today…
myself
God
anyone?

Did I look today…
up above my eyes
into the heart
of others' eyes
into the clouds
of the sky
that exist
outside of imagination
outside of my situation?

Did I connect today...
myself with myself
with God
with anyone
with here and
the ether beyond
with faith and trust
laid in the hand
of the moment
that moved me
to the next
and those
I had yet to stand?

Did I touch today...
the dark in daylight
to voices that
cry in the night?
Did I touch today...
the skin of
my own sin
with the
knowledge
of Jesus
and my Redemptive
Bridge within?
Did I offer hope today...
to myself
to God
to anyone?

Did I allow time to just cope
today...
to myself
to God
to anyone?

Did I laugh, cry, annoy,
quiet, move,
learn anything new,
resist, persist
today?

Did I demand
or unwittingly command
today?
Why?
Why not?
Does this even matter —
it really, only for
a moment,
makes us
seem better...

We can become such nonsense
when our intellect
makes us lose our
innocence...

†††

The loudest most gentle voice
spoke to me from inside —
it whispered
"I need not be heard."

That was when my ego
began to tame

†††

God provides as my dwelling place:
Love; my heart when I
truly slow down my mind enough
to receive its rhythm conveying
messages through emotion, through
breath, through vibration.

Prayer; in direct communion
with our Creator I express <u>Love</u>
through gratitude, through
apologies, through petitions
for peace, healing and comfort
to be bestowed / poured onto
others — others I know
and those I do not; there
I open to God's Wisdom, to
guidance, to my own healing through
forgiveness of another by
lifting them up in prayer, through
forgiveness of myself by remembering
contemplating God's Love shown
to and bestowed upon me through
others and directly through
quiet, visions, dreams, writings,
Mercy and Grace and intuiting
when others are praying for
me — again Love.

12/29/06

†††

God brings me peace
by: reminding me to breathe;
returning me to within
my breath where, eventually,
I become quiet and soothed
as I recognize with gratitude
rather than frustration that
which exists around, outside
of me. When I pray from
that deep place of breath
for others and their needs, (for
my own soul only sometimes —
for when I spend much time
praying for my own I can become
troubled and take myself too
seriously) I find calm in
knowing prayer is heard/received
by God and All in our Holy family
that long only to embrace
our hearts and wait patiently
until we embrace God and
each other as God.
Every time the Father's
language comes through
my pen I am wrapped
in warmth, Love, and comfort
beyond comprehension.

1/11/06

†††

Lord, I know "black or white,"
"all or nothing" is not where You
live. It is where the ego resides (all-white)
and fear hides (black-nothing).
It is where punishment and imperfect-
conditional love breed. Grey is
where true Love, trust and faith
stay. This I know, for when I
let it go — don't plan,
don't question, don't know
which direction, become still
and silent — You place me safely
with Your hands where You
want me.

Grey is where You live.
Grey is Eternity.
Grey is what we don't see,
which is the birth of
hope and true faith
at its maturity.
Forever, Abba, keep us aglow
in the shadow of Your Love.

Amen.

†††

Psychology, theory, people
may look at my "existence,"
my "way," my "emotional
fluctuations" from energetic
sensations, my walking
slowly through the town of process
or running spontaneously
to cross the border and go
with the flow of my
dedication to prayer where
I contemplate
to discern
all
that is out there all
that is in me —
Psychology, theory, people
may look at me as
being "insecure"
Well, I am "insecure"
because I understand
the security in uncertainty.
I have often griped
over not being "logical;"
I have coveted "logic."
Now, I see the
"illogic" in that thinking —
I now understand it was
not for me to be "logical,"
for that would have
skewed the Wisdom, the
gift spoken to and Graced
upon my intuition, my inhibition uninhibited.

Logic could very well
have been a
false sense of protection
a deception that
would have prevented me
from being free to be "insecure"
and survive to live
securely in my insecurity while
knowing so intimately
the only security that exists —
uncertainty —
that fine line of grey
that carries us to guide us
as students as teachers
as Divine revelations
to each other's
Divine mysteries
until we realize
there is no mystery...
It is all Divine
For your reason
For my reason
at some point
the process holds purpose
for all Divinity

1/5/08

†††

Does guilt come from
You or does this branding
come from psychology, or
our own soul's "psyche?"

I guess, probably, it
is a combination. Guilt
that we may think comes from
You really begins in our
soul as it pains over
choices we make that tear
its direction from You,
and for each of us that will
be a different experience.
For what guides this soul
of mine, what binds me
to You in Divine Will
is lovingly unique as it
is for every other child of
Your Soul.

So often psychology,
whether interpreting Your
word, analytical text or
results of study, labels
our behavior and categorizes
our existence —
boxes us in statistics.
Deduced from these
labels, categories and
statistics are created taboos,
shoulds and shouldn'ts, comparisons
to hold against ourselves

—functional / dysfunctional
aware / in denial
controlling / controlled
passive / aggressive
focused / scattered
addicted / recovering
human / purely Holy
...
All of these terms tag us
and lead to judgment
that comes from others'
perceptions around us, or
our own perception of
ourselves based on these
tagging terms — and even,
maybe especially, how
we feel others perceive
us based on those same
terms.
If You are Love
and that Love (You)
births each soul, is it
wrong to believe that guilt
is not of You but rather
from our own soul's
knowing of its denial
of You, of that Love
to receive and of its
own capacity to give
that same Love?

2/7/07

Fill me, Wisdom,
with an intuitive sensitivity
to the needs of others —

who, when, what and for
how long — when to
step aside and give
it back over to You, when
to go where called...
Fill me with an intuitive
sensitivity that hears when
You are speaking to me
through others and the courage
and humility to accept that
which You feel I must hear...

"Wisdom knows when not to
speak...
sings when spoken
for..."

Okay, You are clearly
saying something here...

"True strength comes
quietly...
brings no attention
to itself...
and moves in the
Face of Love"

Intercessory

2/8/07

†††

Don't they understand, realize
what they take away from You, Papa?
Don't they realize how they stand judgmental,
cold and untouchable in their doctrines,
texts on paper and interpretations of Scripture
to form a protective coating around
their existence — a rigid barrier
to interfere with Your reaching through
them out to others?

I suppose what I just wrote
places me in a position of judgmental.
I find after time of feeling surrounded
by those who believe legalistic doctrine
and cherish Scripture as the only way,
I become protective —which can
really be described, I guess, as defensive —
of my own belief that You speak
to all, that You use all, that one
of Christ's most important messages
was that of inner Kingdom —intimate,
personal relationship with You. We are
all in need of embracing our kin-ship
with You, but there is no generic
prescription for this fulfillment. To
follow this way of thinking seems
to me to be contradictory to "the
Kingdom is within." It seems to me
a sedative to cover and quiet what Your
Voice wishes to give us individually
through intimate, contemplative communication
with You. It seems to me this place of
unique relationship is where Wisdom
births in and through us, where we

live our true state of being to
bring forth, just in our very
breath alone, Your being. And in
bringing forth, living this Wisdom,
we (can) offer illumination of
our connection absent of analytical,
protective, defensive, oppressive
separation. When we understand
and appreciate what the "Kingdom
is within" really means —that it is our
beautiful gift from You; when we
understand what it means to us and for
us individually, we can then understand
and appreciate what it means to and
for others —that because we are
unique, "the Kingdom is within" is a
unique and personal experience. In
this we can live the definition of
tolerance, loving tolerance not
tolerance from submission.

Help me, Father, to be
one who lives more and more from
Wisdom and renders patience and
loving tolerance; one who behaves,
reacts, thinks less and less from
defense or judgment and instead
continues to build my Kingdom within
by appreciating and praying for the
same in others.

Breathe Wisdom in me to birth Wisdom through me.

12/21/06

†††

There are no strangers
in God's creation.

†††

Allah Jai Buddha Father
God Jesus Holy Spirit =

No separation
All are One
One is in all
We are all
Holy Spirit
We are all
in God
God is in all —
not only human kind
but ground
grass leaf beetle
cell plankton atmosphere
space and time —
God moves through us
has no distinct look
color size or shape
God is <u>All</u> colors
sizes and shapes
God is not a thought
God is there
whether we think or not...

Love to all
through all
from Above
and back
again

8/06

†††

I heard Jesus tell me
today that when many people
heard "Do for the Glory of God" or
"...to bring Glory to God"
it turns them away, scares
them, jades them, creates fear,
guard or debate.
He told me to continue to
carry out His message rather
"through raising awareness
to Mercy, compassion, understanding,
acceptance and most of all, forgiveness."
For again, He told me "this is Love,
this is Wisdom, this is God. There is only need to be
that Love, and by living this message
we bring ourselves to, and therefore
Glory to, God."

He told me to come to Him
when I lose patience, to just
keep listening for His Voice and
He would restore my trust, my
strength to continue to
live and be that message.
He told me to *"continue*
to recognize and appreciate
others as they live this message,
and others who, because
of fear and hurt, are still
learning."

4/10/07

†††

As souls who seek, is it not more
important what we intend in
what we do in our outreach
than what we preach as we speak?

†††

Narcissism Bubble Syndrome

What would the world and
the humanity it holds be like
if every time we fell into our
states of insecure self-consciousness
we immediately converted those
thoughts into prayer for another?
Rather than be worried or wonder
how we are being perceived by a
you, he or she we could be praying
for a your, his or her heart to
be filled with Love, spirit
to be light and free, soul
to be willed over to God and
anxieties to be eased. This just
might free us of selfish, senseless
concern that only serves to
perpetuate more negative self-
absorption (where we believe we
know what others are thinking; where we
think for them).
We might even free our minds
to open our ears and really be
present with others and what they
are saying to more clearly hear
what is needed of us in those
given moments.

Most likely there would be
substantially more mature honest
relationships with balanced give
and take. We might even enjoy
substantially less crime and
more peace; less false pride
that is bound with fear of
inferiority and therefore, leads to a fight
for superiority. We might quite
possibly experience our created and
creative selves more fully by
turning our souls over to passion
for virtuous Love and Truth, where
we might actually come to rise above
ourselves and catch a glimpse of how
life could be when we move outside
of delusion. Maybe that glimpse
would be enough to fill us with
desire to move in this
way more and more, and as a result, <u>Live</u>
more and more.

5/8/06

†††

How can I still this tongue
from a voice that's
on the run — run
on sentences no pauses
no hesitation —
tangle wrangled
in question
How can I tell You I love You
want to live for Your desire
in my design when
I pray and petition
to grow in virtue
as I dance to fornicate temptation
twist and turn toward every yearn
till again I long and lean
kneeward bound
unveiled face down
Heart's tears cupped in hands
over these eyes
hung to dry in exhibition
Soaked rags of flesh
saturate good intentions...

I'm sorry...

So indulgent...
    Anything want anything had
    18 days into Lent
    haven't sacrificed a thing yet...

So indulgent...
    Not even minutes ten
    devoted to prayer
    where You can speak
    to me of mission in proportion
    to my willing over...

Anything want anything had
Had anything wanted anything
So indulgent
    Consumed in thought
by thought
    Squandered Mercy
    Pranced Glory as inheritance
    Squandered Mercy like Grace is free
        Taking time from giving time
        In neglect I reject Thee.
            I'm sorry...

3/18/06

†††

Gettin' so tired
of hearing what I
have to say
I'm beginning to feel like
just another cliché —

Sometimes think...
    If I have to hear this voice
    one more time
    jump on a soapbox
    or leap off and whine...

Then worry...
    If I sit benign
    I might not slip
    into but out of Your mind
    could become malignant
    and full of contempt
    for the ill eating the ease
    inside of me...

If I turn my eyes
from those words
for too long I wonder
where they'll go   Will I
lose them to someone else
whose countenance
mistakenly attempts but can't
reveal what they meant...

Arent You gettin' tired
of hearing what I have to say
I'm beginning to feel like
just another one of Your clichés...

Walkin' this road of fortitude
just lookin' for a warm spot
under an intimate sun
where I can raise my feet
from this effusive, redundant
underground
sit a while and meditate
on my still tongue...

I'm sorry...

3/06

†††

In traveling for You
I've traveled too far
again   far away   miles
away from You   I
look and choke
cause all I see
is haze fog and haze

Used to be Your Eyes
the lines in Your Face
to light the night clear
and settle me   Settle
(me) for a little   Here
I'd find my breath
from wind in Your Voice
Gentle rushing waters
to cool me off
from the heat of thought
Your palm strong over
my slouching shoulder...
I cry to You   Why
You already know
the salt to that doubt
confusion and sorrow
Longing to do right   yet
wronging in wondering
lost in wandering...

or is it then I am
found in Listening
as I glide along
Your Hand in mine
to guide my "here
there and everywhere"
as I go   return
and go to return
always within because I'm
moving out without
limit minute to minute
nothing minute nothing grand
All is Sacred
All is Sacred...

Is it
Sacred to live as wind
Is it
there I am never far
there You are   You are
never far... my chattering
overwhelms my sight dim...

6/2/06

†††

Life is not constant
Slippery when wet
Brittle when dry
It is smooth bland
and sweet burning
fire-gold-amber

It is ledge-on-the
edge fragile
Incomplete
circumstantial
emotion melting thoughts
of words that compete
in opposite
should
should not
absence
presence
that
this
here
gone
never
over

Words
label
subtle to extreme
Name it this
Create a that
If not that
it must be this

We have given life over
to words that label
(form belief systems)

clouding choices
in battling voices
"I should
should not
I would
would not"
clouding choices
from where Life grows
in everything
that moves between
shadow vision
sketch photograph
taking giving
reality perception
Perception...
confusion or
wondering?
Lost or .
roaming ?
Lost or .
exploring ?
Lost . .
finding ?
Lost . .
living ?

Give up quit
or
give up give away ?

1/29/07

†††

Life is learning how to live
over and over again...

Letting go inviting in —
Letting go
open — shut — open

Risk — mistake —
Risk — mistake

Uncover — recover
Uncover

Hello — goodbye
Hello

Letting go — inviting in
Letting go

Life is learning to live
over and over again

because life is learning to love
— over and over again
whether a new or "ever unchanging" someone
whether another or heart of our own...

4/17/07

†††

Do I love myself enough
to love You more than
I love myself, Father?

Or do I still hold onto
too much selfishness that
blocks or inhibits my reaching
the level of love that is
within my fullest capacity;
selfishness that keeps me
from sharing that love to
then inhibit my full experience
of You?

If I truly love myself,
should I love You more than
me? For the more I love You
the more I see You in others,
in life all around me.
In loving others and life
all around me I move in time
with You — I move in
"Time that does not pass, but grows."

But Your Holy Spirit, She
is within me, so should I
not look at the depths of our
love comparatively? For how can
I say I love You more and
love me less if You are
within me? How can I
say I am not worthy to love
myself as I love You, as You
Love me, when a piece of
Your creation has become me?
Should I rather just come to
You inside (of me) gratuitously
from where I recognize and
humbly appreciate Your Love,
any love, others love —
loving Love?...

11/16/06

†††

Too many influences in our culture hold to a system of never enough — that enough is complacency and complacency is sin. When is enough enough? When is enough not enough? When is enough too much? Why is enough not allowed to be enough?

True spirituality, Love, living from the soul is not easy, but it is simple. It requires only awareness, gratitude and giving mind and body over to Spirit to move and love from the heart. The heart's function is tremendous, it never sleeps. Yet, its means to achieve its function remain simple — that is until we complicate matters.

God's Spirit, God's existence in us remains simple, ever present, and is only absent in our delusion — when we complicate matters by maintaining a view of a God that exists <u>only</u> outside of ourselves — outside of the body. We push God further away as we extend flailing arms and hands trying to grasp at ideals, doctrines and fretful thoughts that continue to seek for what the dissecting

mind believes is far reaching
and requires definitive absolutes
to be achieved...
    "Oh God what is it You
    want me to do?!
    What is my calling?!..."
Our calling is to love God with all
of our mind, our body and our spirit
— the three properties of the
soul — memory, understanding and
will — gathered in His name. And
to love our neighbor as ourselves,
knowing we are created in the image
of our Creator and that it is good.

†††

Simple steps seek not
to know all the answers
at once,
but find profound existence
in the question of every moment's
touch...

†††

Why must we turn
    gifts of the Divine
    into such beasts?
    Those with these
        idolize?
Why must we glamorize
    the angelic?
Why are we so "above"
    the mundane...
    everything grand
        and more grandiose yet?
Why must we all be heroes?
Why must we all be Jesus
    while we dispute, forget
    who He was in what He did,
        in what He said?
Why are we so afraid
    to forgive?
Why must we always win —
    so afraid to lose
    and come undone...
Why must everything be competition?

Why must we fear
    illness, aging...
    be made to feel
    it is a sin?
    Is it not more so
    to fight nature
    is to sin?
Why must we take
    what is beautiful
    and rob it of its beauty
    turn it ugly...
    and what is harmfully ugly
    raise to desirable?
Why must we pretend
    to be solid,
    sane and joyful?

†††

So much emphasis on what we
look like — physical appearance; on
what we say — how intelligent,
entertaining, knowledgeable; on what we
do — performance, achievements, awards,
recognition...

I just want to enjoy eye contact,
touch, dance — to feel the energy
and pain-free ability to move my legs,
arms and hips — to be able
to breathe fresh air from lungs
and a stomach that do not hurt
constantly, to not have to stress
over the pain of eating, the pain
of not going to the bathroom. Some days, I just
want to enjoy energy to sit outside
in the grass without worrying, "Will I
be able to get up?"
I just want to have the
energy to awake and take a shower without
the fatigue that comes from temperature
change reaction, to not have to keep track
of doctor appointments, medical treatments, medicine
and financial assistance.

I am not crying for pity. I am
crying because it hurts me to
see how much is taken for granted
and the grand emphasis placed
on ownership, acclaim, fame, housing,
vehicle, material aspirations and
even the desire for perfection
in things unbroken to begin with.

3/29/07

†††

My highest aspirations at this
given moment?

To become skin that
covers a set of hand
drums and feel
the palms of other souls

To realize my dream
of sleeping upon
a leaf
and wake with my cheek
kissing green silk
rise as dew
glisten
and wait
for the eye of the moon
as I then curl
up fetal
again

3/25/07

†††

My deepest desire
is indescribable
for words would lay her
dark-hole-
pigeoned Bruised
wings under skin

My deepest desire
wears no color
and smokes no fire
for she has no view
for perception
no lungs
to taste resin

My deepest desire
rests in the Womb
and drinks the
Liquid Sound
of Wisdom...

12/21/06

†††

The process of processing
has gone on its way...

With nothing at all
to say, not a word...

Not even "good bye"
or "see you in a while"...

...from so many
who had too much
"something"
to speak???
shshhhhhhhhhhhh...

Liquid Sound
of Wisdom

4/11/07

†††

Dryness can sometimes become a "moist oasis" to quench our spiritual longing — our thirst for Christ's Eyes upon our own in reflection, and for intimacy with God — that in times of quiet or in times of chaos and great need brings us to rediscover Abba. We are always in opportunity to rediscover Jesus Love and teaching and the Holy Spirit's Voice — our closest friend — through Her <u>breeze</u> <u>or</u> <u>wind</u> that whispers Wisdom into our souls from our great one tree of infinite good, infinite Love and Mercy.

I thank You, Father, for offering me the <u>many</u> opportunities to peek through the Eyes of Mystical experience, as well as those times of nary ice chips to my chapped, dry lips.

I thank the Holy Spirit's unfaltering companionship, the Holy Spirit's persistence as counsel when so fraught with dolorous ennui,' in spells of blindness, I could not see this Beacon calling me to the Well. Yet even when my vision is poor, rhythm off and spirit sore, silently — whether in rabid race or subtle stroll — this Beacon has always, will always bring me to that Well...

That Well that springs
from Jesus' Face
and rains over to reveal
and Mystify my soul
so bestowed glimpses
into and through
the Eyes of Yahweh
to give rise to lessons
in self-awareness   Eyes
that fill my cup with
                    liquid Mercy
until, again, I glean
self-less-ness
until fluent
in His language
    of Love
I know where there is no
self there is no one alone
where there is no one alone
there is no loneliness
Until fluid
in the movement of prayer
I breathe in to bathe in
deep-shallow-high-low
thunderous-lightening
struck-tear-streaked
waves peaked that tip-toe
trickle down in soft-current
                                flow
                          of intercession

Where I find to identify me
as no specific person or thing
but indistinguishable
from purpose, from need
of all other
Where I step to steep
in the tempo
of one-unified-God-world-soul...

3/27 - 28/06

In gratitude of the incredible Mystical experience my life has been. As well, in aspiration of becoming no-one special while still integral to the whole — a clear, open, unobstructed vessel.

†††

Salvation — Love for and of the soul;
Love for and of Creator;
Love for and of creation
in every creature;
Longing of a soul to
see all other souls
experience this filial Love

†††

Red Rock Rind

I want to peel
    Your red rock rind
and swim in the Core
    of Your clay land
To know what it is
    to come undone
Erode in the arid
    parched pit of Your
canyon to climb on
(in) that hematite heart
holding Your brush of
    terracotta paint
decorate my
    delicate face
and surface as petroglyphs
    dancing in the threads
of Your canvas

9/21/01

Driving through canyon lands of Utah
So much red rock

†††

Bryce Canyon, Utah
photo by Kimberlyann DeAngelo

So far from Home...
So far from I...

I close my hollow
eyes... shed a desert cry...

Dig for the well
in the deep
of my hell
and drink in the flame
of a devil as he
burns to reap
Holy water he takes
from my sane mind
once fed
perfectly by Lord of thine...

I close my hollow
eyes... shed a desert cry...

I dream this secret...
a movie inside
making love to my mind

I ride its reel
come full circle
in loyalty

attempt no edit
as I protect
where I live
peacefully

As I am meant...
an island
reached only through
prayer expecting no answer
and looking within

I close my hollow
eyes... shed a desert cry...

I am in the Arms of...

a Gaze that meets
mine — penetrates
flesh and bone
I come undone

a Look that calls
my demons
unconscious to rile
my sobriety
and dive into this
bottle of Intimacy

want I want
I don't want
to deny that
licks my lips
to moisten this
Oasis...

I float in this Space
away from hell into Sensual
and wonder if I can sip
and sustain or will
I take it all in
at once drunk again
intoxicated run oblivious
to cork but empty remains —
my empty remains...

I close my hollow
eyes... shed a desert cry...

Gypsy
my gypsy soul
"Blue River"
Where do you wanna go
you always wanna go
girl
Always pull
never let me settle
We tail spin
on Your whim
we're gonna expire
in Your desire

Maybe that's the answer

You're frustrating
exhilarating
Your temptation
is exhausting...

You wanna ride on snow
melt as moisture
into fertile soil

F
a
l
l as dew
on a leaf
ready to lift
and twirl
float away
evaporate
in the sun
Fly on a bug and
ride the tendrils
of wind
Crawl on wood
bark thin
ready to peel
move on and on

I love hate You
cause I can't leave
You You get in the way
of focus of Love
You become
my Lover

I need You
tried so hard
to tame You
bring You into me

Blue River

Now let me bring
myself into You

I'm beginning to understand
You
are
God
dancing within
I want to slip
into Your dress
Kiss my feet
to Your grass
Sing chant
from the breast
of my heart
until my voice
touches Your lips...

"Walk on the water"
You say I *"won't drown"*
This I should know
for I have been saved
You have saved me
4 times or so...

My maiden can't see
for the mist of yesterday
where waters crash and rise
too high to fall
from her mind —

Tread is what she wants
but trips instead
spins as the whirlpool
pulls her in

Her gaze might quit
but hope on wings
brings her back above
skyward in the Face
of Love
till stillness of her
body motionless
floats like a
raft through her
giving the water
chance...

She lives...

immune to expectation
maintains who she is
Leads the child her own
(who cannot conform)
to kneel and pray
at the alter within...

Rises to the feet of
scorned dismay —
camouflaged-fear-raised
eyebrows daggering
to catch her —
fills her shaker of
salt and pepper
with greying ashes
and turquoise tears
cried over
to feed shallow waters
of souls lost from sea...

She walks...

blue-green eyes
toward indigo
and draws
purple skies
orange-yellow

Feet dream
soft sand
unstrapped so
overall
music finds
her desert rose

Dancing petals
life moves
her gypsy soul...

I close these eyes
of blue-green

Green-blue tapestries
of a Mind not of mine
come into view

Tapestries woven in passing
colors that move through
sunsets of lips in sand
beaches of bones...

life after death

Life

†††

church in Sedona, Arizona
photo by Kimberlyann DeAngelo

River That Once Was

Flowing river,
take me under
current of Your spell.
Don't leave me in Your wishing well.

Water of blood so pure,
think I've been here before,
like mother's womb
from where You bloom,
lullabied
in ebb and tide
of a heart beating true
so connected to You.

Markings of Your Presence
on rocks remaining,
baring Your Essence
sketching the painting
to past existence.

Flowing river,
take me under
that spell
don't leave me in Your wishing well.

Carry me there, to where
I rediscover
who I've been
another life within,
etching out who I am.

Heaven or Hell,
I want to know.
Not afraid to go
and search that soul,
river that once was
feeding this life's cause.

When I move on,
cross the other side,
will it be the end
or a turning tide?
Will more to learn
bring me back
time after time
'till demons I lack
and "Divine-True," I earn?

Flowing river,
drank Your potion,
I'm drunk in motion
craving for more.
Under Your spell...
Don't leave me in Your wishing well.

(Sitting on rocks in Sedona, Arizona mountains,
acknowledging river that once flowed in a time
long gone. Felt strong connection, presence of
spiritual aspects from the time past.
So soothing, yet simultaneously invigorating.
Was my spirit here before —
a life lived as another?)

†††

Darkness switched
on the Light
Trembling shook
me still
as tears
soaked me dry
and cold I fell
in to His warmth.

Love
would not
let me die.
Why?

"My daughter, no,"
He said,
"you are not done.
Proof that I am
you did not need.

Your love My Face
did gain.

I've told you
I give your neighbor
for you to know love
you can.

I've told you
this is to return
your love to Me.
But, in asking you
to know Me,
I am asking
you believe
in My Love
of and for
you.
This is faith
in Me.

So many questions.
They, so many
question Me.
Now let Me ask,
why?

My beloved flower
your spirit will share
what you have seen.
You mustn't be timid —
My Hand in yours
you were raised.
I,
your Beloved,
will be loved
through your eyes,
your touch
and words
spoken through these.

I
your Beloved
will be loved
through your
love
remembered
in My Name."

10/06/06, 2:00 A. M.

Awoke with this in my ears after
falling asleep remembering my N.D.E.
from suicide attempt, asking God to
speak, praying that I be a clear, free channel.

†††

I am having another near
death experience, only this time,
without the death...
I hear sound in colors
so vibrant and pure
that linger my eyes
to see hearts that beat
in movement flowing
ever so still —
Beautiful —
So many visions of late
Signs in dreams waking me
feeling awake in my sleep
Yearning always this yearning
that yearns me
Nausea from hunger
for nourishment
from the elements
not for want
of anything
claiming "tangible"
Waking with my body
on a leaf in my mind's eye
Feeling the "work" of prayer
my prayer Your prayer
Responding directly to my calling
upon Your comfort —
Mercy, You soothe me
Nothing matters but <u>Love</u>
So many faces all the same

in <u>every</u> expression, <u>Love</u>
wants only to give and receive
Love, not of this world, Your longing
in mine has finally taken me
and here, not of this world,
I am with You, Lord,
in this world
and together, You in I,
can bring Love
from pine on the mountain
down to seeds
and water them
in every breath we breathe
Your "wild flower meadow"
is my field of dreams
It is where I lie down
to shower and roll under
to cover my skin
until my body is only figment
of my imagination
from which

Your Imagination
    is where I draw
    to dare not need to imagine...
I flicker in Your candle, Lord,
    until You wax over me...
(content, gracefully content)

†††

Portal to Another

Mystic ships
        traveling realms of existence
chambers open
        fasten us in
                        loose
Drenched in freedom
        bound in "can't break away"
Discover another door
        portal to another   room
        sensation pulls in —
                        trigues
We follow whispers beneath

Immersed
        Approach upon-reverent-
        in sweetest descent
        dip, dip in —
                        herent

waters rise
suspend us poised
in Eyes of dewy seas
Bed in waves
on hands of wings
to draw a glimpse
of life beyond this
ocean chrysalis...

2/16 &18/06

Near death experience. Souls traveling,
levels, meetings, dreams.

†††

Responsive
perceptive
sentient
fragrant
mellifluous
melodious
splendid
exquisite
euphonious
exquisite
splendid
melodious
mellifluous
fragrant
sentient
perceptive
responsive

6/18/06

†††

Oh God, it's You again.

Do You have to keep
knockin' on my door?

Every time I let You in
I fall on my knees
to the floor
aware of my self-
conscious conscience
aware of my ego
choosing will

I just wish to sleep
a bit
vege like a piece
of lint
in a worn
pocket...

1/12/07

†††

Is there a devil
or,
is there only free will?

(While on a walk
moon on my left
sun to my right
came upon an oasis
a park full with trees
that danced so gracefully
sang to me as they
took my hand and
invited me in...)

3/25/07

†††

I know You Love me
and want only my pure
uncluttered love and
sanctification. I know, too,
that I have always prayed
to be raised out of self,
above and into You, to be
raised in transformation and
sanctification. I asked for
more simplicity, a cave in
which I could dwell to hear
Silence Profound. Did I
know what I was asking for?
Did I know what my soul
still needed to learn, to
empty of, to suffer, to mourn?
Maybe. Probably. But was I
really ready? Maybe. Probably.
For after blood on my lip formed
a crucifix on the napkin and
Mary showed herself to me laying
her arm, chest and face across
my stomach, I no longer felt
I had any choice —that my
soul would no longer let me
choose. Yet, even still I fight,
complain and cry like a brat
throwing tantrums not wanting
to comply.

You are my journey
You are my love
You are my thorn
You are my agony
You are my heart
You are my eyes
If upon receiving
my beggar's plea —
what I pray
and pray for —
I lament
rather than
graciously repent,
I am sorry
for any lies
in those thoughtless
requests...
I do want to be continually
raised, to see me through
my own eyes in Your Light.
I wish I could do this
without grieving all the loss
of what my mind
perceived as a win
before.
I truly wish I could
lay down distraction
and torment once
and for all...

Yes, I do want
it to be easier,
less details
that derail.
But I know,
sometimes distraction
is unavoidable
and is more so
part of the lesson
of the moment
and it is only
my perception
that sees it as otherwise.

I just wish I could discern each experience
for its necessary lesson
or my rebellion
before it becomes
past tense.

12/9/07

†††

You should never have
seduced me
harnessed me so
I have become selfish
possessive
in wanting You
all for only
the depth of my well
to feed and flow
from here
You call, lure me
as You Love
and I ache
to be Holy
But the more You touch
the more I look

at me

and I used to love
to share
Oh, how this "looking"
creeps "narcissistic"
You have uncovered
to discover in me
a jealous lover
—territory I never did
taste before —how
could this deem
Holy?

I talk so much of Your
experience
in me, for it is
encouragement
But encouragement
be what they take?
I cannot know
—for it must seem
bent on "boast"
to glorify my soul
I have never known in me to own
possessiveness
of another
only upon me to be
suffocated, frayed
from manipulation
in its obsession
How can I forgive myself
for the sufferance
I lay upon
as I treat You
the way others
have treated me —
as an object
of possession?

I'm sorry

8/18/08

†††

Oh Lord, fertilize
this flower's soil,
aerate to spread my roots
among those whose souls
weep, feel lost or confused
to show them Your hand
and the beauty in
their own being —
the beauty of God,
the Great Sky that cries
over our minds...

†††

Not too long ago
I said,
"I brought my Love
to bed with me...
that was my first mistake
Then I closed my eyes
and went to sleep...
Now I wait upon
my heart to wake..."
Lover, my Lover
why so lightly
did You tuck
me in so tight
without even
a kiss goodnight?
Soft-footed and smooth,
instead You laid me down
in this kiss-of-death
heart ache
"For" my "own good,
to better know" my "self,"
You said

But so much time
in these sheets of guilt
sheets of sin and will...
I've seen it all
before, again, already...
There is no more
to know of me
of self
of I am
I am no less
of who I was
no more
of who I am...
Toss and turn,
I can't even...
Your absence
leaves me listless
Don't leave me here
in limbo
weeping to wilt
until again
in saliva of You, Your kiss
I melt...

12/9/07

†††

May the Sweetness of My Peace Embrace You

"I know how you feel
walking into walls
whatever direction you move...
I know what it means
to see the Light
and wish you hadn't,
for then you'd not know
the dread beholden in
darkness that reappears
despite all efforts
of resilience your
spirit holds —
Trust, hope... lose their appeal
as restless slumber
lusts for sleep
while awake...
I know your fragile heart
raw in break, pure
for sake of who?
for sake of what?
I know your weakness
in your strength
of traveling alone,
afraid to drag another
down

afraid to see the soul
of another
again
and so in and in
your eyes, once
the depths of Life,
sink further in disbelief,
further vacant
in a stare that yearns
to forget the need
to communicate
Light...
I know your experience
that regrets the future
before it becomes your past...
And I know your courage
that continues to
step outside and wear
who you are for all
knowing the chances
branding will befall
you again...
I know your sadness
that suffers in empathy
inside of you
for others, for Me

I know your grieving of
all the loss
and the purpose it holds
yet to be disclosed
as you struggle
with maintenance along
the ambiguous nature
My road reveals...
You only need to remember
My Love is always
with you
and in this Love
you are always
where you need
to be and with Me
you are always
who you are
meant to be
And in the sweetness
of My Peace you
will again be embraced..."

I Love You, Papa,
but I have been here so many
times before and wonder
if it wouldn't be better to not
know You so well...

For this game of showing Yourself
to me clearly, vividly
and then hiding only to increase
my longing,
only to confuse
my understanding
of why You've held
onto me so tightly,
I don't know that I
can play anymore...
(You show me a door then You
close it???)
...for at times it seems
this game is killing me
and I don't know why
You trust me so much
and I don't believe
I can carry this
weight of this cross
anymore...
For I was old before I was young
and I'm sorry, but
now I just want to play
and mosey along

†††

"A thirsty river runs dry
attempting freedom
in directions unending...
Lost in its way
wanders adrift
travels and shifts
to advance its trip.
Any passage to tantalize
draws attention, scatters
matter from what matters
now seeking Providence
burning barren, cries to the
mouth of its Source —
'Find me where I am.
Seep to me!
Bleed to me!
Feed me!'"

Ocean Mother waves
in tender Voice,
"Come a little closer
My wayward searcher
— outstretched —

Limitless perceived limitations
circle, spurn to turn
a dirty needle in your back
that twists into muscle inflexible
as another tear — tears drawn
come to surface in mirrored cracks...

Let Me blow you a kiss
to catch your eye,
repeace your faith.
Let Me reach your veins
and feed your understanding
under My affection.

In fresh water blue
I'll blanket you
to flow compassionate
from My compassion —
a rivulet not separate.

Spin yourself free — a lover
to rise over, walk outside the circle
and cross through the Eyes of
Mercy into each other."

4/27/06

†††

This season of suffering
is / was to raise my soul
out of delusion by making me
aware of my imperfect love —
love of consolation — and of
spiritual selfishness. This season
is / was as well, to gift me
Wisdom that helps me to reflect
and understand Wisdom's gifts
throughout my life. This season
of dryness is / was to help me
grow a more beautiful flower
of compassion that stems
from True Holy Desire for
virtuous sensuality and
charity.

Help me, Jesus, to endure
and come to moisture in the
pasture of humble and intercessory
prayer. Wrap around me to
wrap around others.

2/07

†††

Rivulet Compassionate

I pray ABBA, to be a mermaid
whose pores drink and breathe
in beads of Your sweat
that feed to fill earthly seas
from the Ocean Divine...

Love they who I am with
through me
Show through them
myself in capacity
to realize a Love
that will not
anesthetize...
Love that lifts my heels
from this surface
To raise my eyes in affection
where I come to kiss
our Lord's feet and
taste Love's blood
pure-blue-poured-red-sweet
And at His feet
drink Love's blood
pure-blue-poured-red-sweet...

If not a mermaid, may I
  spring to fill any cup
  with tears from my well
  that carry galaxies of hope
  to quench despair

  where I may ebb and flow
  below to let them soar —
  mend a broken wing
  and ask for only nothing
  more than a hand
  that bears to bare
  witness my ego weaker
  than soul for in me
    You hung Yours
    He hung His
    in the balance
    of free will...

Here, a rivulet compassionate,
    I will eat dust from toes
    of other one's journey
    and savor to honor
    any parched pass
    of hill-scourged agony
    so came to overcome
    affliction wounding

3/1, 4/8/06

†††

Mercy can know no time for rest.
Compassion cannot close its eyes
on a collective soul
bearing wounds so severe.
It must maintain faith in her
good, in individual good;
faith in individual-intent-ill
longing to turn around unbound
from evil learned, to
bring that soul to consciousness.

For in the house
of self-knowledge
it sits constant in watch —
remains aware, "There,
but for the Grace of God,
go I."

5/20/06

†††

Father, help me to walk what
I say, to be what I pray.
Help me to come to You with
All of me, to remove any veil,
for I need no guard in Your
Presence. It is not You who
threaten my existence, but
You who make it possible to be;
You who breathe life through me.
Help us to truly understand
the Holy Spirit, Its capacity for
intimacy. Help us to know Your
omnipresence in that breath no
matter how stressed, preoccupied,
tucked far away we may feel.
Please do not refrain from speaking
through us, nor dancing in us.

Forever, Abba, keep us aglow
in the Shadow of Your Love...

Amen

3/14/05

†††

The closer I move toward You, Father,
the further from myself I escape.
As I look back over the years of
journals, poems and philosophical
thoughts, I become ever increasingly
aware not a thought, nor prayer,
went by You. You heard every
word on those pages — pages
that came from tears trapped in a
heart longing to melt. Every reflection
brings me to a deeper understanding
of how You work, how You teach,
how You Love —You were my only
constant.

To bring us closer to You, to the "other
side;" to save us from ourselves, You
slowly strip us of every mask,
every persona, every idea we
think we own. You slowly bring
us outside-in to show us our
disguise(s), our notions of what we've
become — our "egodentities" walking
our trails while the "God-childentity"
sleeps, screams, paces in its man-made
cage.

With the gift of Your Grace
You show us how to, and that we can,
shed that ugliness to instead reflect
our Truth —Your Light. Yet, You
know us so well, You give us Your
Hand while allowing us the illusion
hands of our "own" are working the
clay, spinning the wheel and chipping
away to inside out. In Love's Way,
in Love's Time, self-less Holy Spirit
is revealed to the grateful child
of innocence and awe in timely
and harmonious reunion.

Thank You, thank You
Amen

4/25/05

†††

Come upon me like lightening
thunder my world
Take my heart in Your lips
Stroll in my soul
inhale, exhale
through my eyes
sighs of my eyes
Stream my conscience clean
Render me free
In Your grasp
I quiver
gasp under tender
Mercy ecstasy
(descend, ascend)
in Your touch.

1/24/06

†††

Make Love to me, Jesus...
Raise me from
this bed of ground
where my feet
tied and bound
arch, not to touch,
upward from the earth...

12/12/06

†††

I am God's child
God's daughter...
I am, when He plays
with me, Jesus'
sister...
His lover, when He
confides in me.
His lover, whenever
His blood kisses me...
I am Jesus' mother
when He needs
comfort, acknowledgment
His suffering was not
in vain,
His Love upon us
not wasted;
when anguish streaks
His Face
I kiss those tears
and tell Him
if I could I would
take away His pain,
how sorry am I
I could not protect Him
from His Father,
from murder,
but His Father
could see much
further than human
eye

showed us grief
to show us Life
And
there is no protection
great enough
to withstand
the Love
of God

11/28/07

†††

Compassionate

Humble

Restorative

Inspirational

Sensitive selfless student

Thoughtful tolerant teacher

9/17/06

†††

I do not wish to imitate
Christ. Many of us can imitate,
ape, mimic etc... But this can
be just like putting on an
outfit or a hat for a moment.
Does it really enter into
us to then come from our
depth of truth, or just rest
on our surface to create an
appearance or image.
Maybe for some
by mimicry they eventually do
come to feel and believe what
they wear, what they imitate.
I pray rather than imitate
Christ, I find Christ within
myself on an ever growing
walk toward willing my soul
in whole over to Father. And
that in so doing I become more
as Christ lived from the depths

of my truth — for this
Love and Life to be my truth,
not an imitation. I pray
rather than be concerned about
imitating Christ, I become
more and more intimate with
Him and that means for me inviting
Him into my thoughts, my eyes,
my words, my heart, my breath and
my partaking in conversation with
Him as someone who is always
with me. I pray to become more
and more of a soul that needs
less and less of self, more of a place
where if Christ would come today
He could find a peaceful rest.

2/17/07

†††

It is interesting, sometimes
can be very lonely and strange,
how the closer Christ moves
into one's experience, the closer
one moves toward Christ in that
experience, the further away
move others from that one...
Could it be that one who
experiences this intense
intimacy also experiences
the suffering and sacrifice
of Jesus — (sacrifice —
Mercy, compassion, <u>empathy</u> — Life),
and others do not understand
or are afraid to face suffering
or truly contemplate this experience?

Why are people so afraid?
They talk of "feeling," "observing"
this "Light," "connection," "Spirit"
"in and with" that one. Yet, they
gradually move away or distance
themselves quickly. Why do they
draw from this "Light," comment

as to recognition of this "Light," then
hide from it? Why does it intimidate?
It only wants to illuminate so to
share the "Light." It never wants
to scare, overwhelm, condemn etc...
For one with this "Light" needs to
share so to shed, otherwise, this one
may be completely consumed and
overwhelmed themself... and the "Light"
knows this...

Please don't fear (Me) me
Please don't wonder about (Me) me
Please don't compare yourself to,
    nor judge yourself by (Me) me
Please only accept what
    this "Light" has to offer
    if it is in your need
Please only share in (My) my Grace
    for it is far too much
    to keep for (Myself) myself and
    carry alone

†††

Tender passionate Lover
thoughtful so thoughtful,
soft and easy
undemanding
giving sharing open
to let me rest
and remain
unguarded
sexy so sweet
and smooth...
His touch is the ocean,
that soothes where I stand,
tenderly washing over
my feet on the warm
and sturdy wet sand
of His arms around me.
I look up into His Eyes
that come inside, become
one with mine. Eyes
that see my heart,
that taste and flavor
my dreams and travel
my soul to feel
my prayers
and speak thoughts —
my thoughts without words.

I want to be His flower,
His rainbow, rhythm of harmony, a prayer.

I want to be arms
        that take Him Home...
I want to be His instrument,
                His pillow,
                His second wind...
I carry Him in my heart
where the eyes of my soul
see the gift that He is.

6/4/06

†††

Love is...
        The hand of God on one's skin.
Love is...
        The heart of God in one's eyes.
Love is...
        God's laughter in the joy of 2 together.
To live the magical Mystery of one's Soul mate in
one's lifetime is Divine.

12/05

†††

Thank You, Wisdom

They told me this,
            the leaves
If I listened
    to the whitness of
            their whisper
            the Sky
            would call me under
            the sea of Her waves

I did — I listened
    and found myself
    inside my Heart

4/5/07

†††

Love
that Loves
spirit winged

twirls as moments
unfold unfolds
from palms
a continuum
unfolds from
palms that seek no
alms...

12/4/06

†††

The Love shown to me through the two souls who
conceived me has been, is today,
the intricate thread that
has kept me connected to what
Love is, connected to the beautiful
gift of Unconditional Love —
which is what Grace is. The
love of my two parents has been,
is today, the intricate thread
that has taught me to love
outside of myself; to seek to
understand, and fill my belly
with the water of compassion
released in tears of prayers
to quench the hearts of those
misunderstood — the hearts
of those who feel they stand
judged and alone, which is
a pair of shoes we have all
worn or will stand in at
some point in our lives.
The love of my two parents
has kept me connected to the
knowledge we are born with
— to love Love — and
the memory of that which is
Eternal.

12/28/06

†††

What happens to those moments
that lie between our memories —
moments to which we become estranged?

What happens to the spaces
        that lie between the beats
                        of our heart?

Is this where the moments
        between memories escape,
        locked in a box of hope
        in a chest that catches breaths
        before we lose — to keep
        us in — control?

"Who took your childhood
made you tuck your toys away
in dreams inside your head,
told you there wasn't any time for play?

Who pegged you inadequate,
        told you you weren't any good
        if you weren't all good?

You don't have to prove yourself
to Me. Just show Me some
humility and I'll dress
naked in your duress;
I'll be your never ending
eden-petal-silk-rose garden.

Swallow some pride for Me
and I'll come down upon
cold fruit
to press warm-juice-
deep colors that ferment
proof fine — I'll be
the one to drink your grapevine
into wine."

5/8/06

†††

I am about to walk
off and away again. This time,
once and for all... into
the wilderness of Wisdom, the
wilderness of my soul.
Find me the cave, Lord,
where I can experience
this communal sound of
Silence Profound
and come to sing in echo
with animal
unclothed
unveiled...

Amen

6/15/07

†††

"Walk out on sin
into the arms of redemption.
A Love that never ends..."

I take a walk through You
and find myself
from all I thought I knew
Indigo tears fall on down
thirsty skin
to feed
color
my wild
flower
meadow
in bloom again

Apart
I am without

You whisper from trees
Call me near

I reach out longing needles
of pine in evergreen desire
And know that You are
The rhythm I dance in
the heat to my valley
my prayer unspoken

You are textures of my soul
once covered in the fabric
of forgotten

Amen

1/23/06

†††

Every day, every hour,
every minute is alive
in stimuli that moves
every language of the body
to share a story

Every day, every hour,
every minute is alive
in stimuli to sting
the senses of a mind fertile
that seeks to indulge
in hope as it walks
through a kaleidoscope
of pollination
in steps merging colors
emerging
instruments tuned to dreams
of uncovered secrets to play songs
that speak in waves of sound
direction to ripple the effect
of Life continuing — Life meeting
life, of Life holding all
to One Connection.

5/19/06

†††

Creation occurred in fragments...
each piece brought forth to God
what would further enhance the
masterpiece. It seems as if God
did not have an ultimate picture
in mind, but allowed for each day
(moment) to inspire the next layer of
beauty, of idea, of imagination, of
need for what would miraculously
work to support individual identity
— individual function — as a
whole of ultimately inseparable parts.

This concept or truth is what we need
to contemplate from our memory,
our reason and our hearts to remain
humble and strive for the reunion
of <u>all</u> humanity with <u>all</u> of creation
— especially human upon human
and Creator. When we maintain this
reason and knowledge we naturally
create visions of beauty through love
presented in word, touch, thought,
prayer, presence, deed, service,
stillness, gratitude and patience.

1/1/08

†††

Sam asked, "Where do you
think you will go when you
die?"

My reply, my prayer —

"I will be here in the
intangible space that cries,
that smiles between the
physical spaces. I will be
in the intuition that whispers
and speaks between the
voices of thoughts. I will
be in the oxygen, the
subconscious breaths of
consciousness to touch and
guide those souls still
bound to earthly existence
and struggling, growing, moving
through their heart's lessons
— just as so many spirits have
done for me in this lifetime's turn.
I will become to give
what has been shown to me
through Mercy and Grace,
again and again —
I will become to give Mercy
and Grace.

I will exist in the Soul of Collectiveness
with one hand held to the
Source of Its (our) center
while extending my hand
remaining to those in this
tangible world so they may
relearn and know their own
connection to that of Supernatural,
their naked and unmasked beginning;
so they may live in the
awareness that we are all
pieces of each other.

We are all pieces of each
other whether still
living to die in our flesh-
toned capsules or dying
to live on the wings of
our spirit that crosses
over."

9/5/06

†††

If I knew tomorrow were
my last breath, how
would I spend tonight?

In mother's arms
tracing her face
kissing her heart...

In father's arms
dancing on his feet
kissing his heart...

Then from Beautiful
who birthed me here
out I would glide
to Beloved's arms
into the Eyes of (His) wilderness
where the rain speaks to me
taps my shoulder
in Love's saliva
dissolves me in rapture
as I nymph to fairy
and fly like a dragon
under the heart
of the moon
and rise
to her vision

My body a body no more
my body no-body no form
from His soil no earth
no idea no ideal
no heaven no hell
mars into venus
no mars no venus
one from two worlds
Beloved
no ground between us...

8/28/0

†††

"Traveling lover
be still
lay down for just a while
clouds will soothe
burning sun
upon eyes so sore
when Love's saliva
rains to kiss
your shoulder again
just lay there
Lay down
Lay down

Lay down in the rain..."

Thank You, Father,
Great One Feminine

Mud upon skin
I cleanse myself
fill my palms
with lathered kisses
that roll me in
leaves that change
me colorful over stains...

3/15/07

†††

Papa,
All these miles walked
trialled journeys
scorched...
Seeking to understand only to explain...
My "reason for being here"
has finally found its reason
in just waiting,
as I speak only through listening.

My voice communicates,
knows its peace,
among the animals, insects,
birds and trees.

Though I wait in the breath
of this earth
my body is done here
for my soul is already Home.

5/9/07

†††

A benevolent Source
spoke to me a long time
ago... showed me in a
vision of beauty and an
experience of life's fragility
where to come for a
breath of strength...

This Source left me
with the message that
I needn't fear for anything;
that Love will always
care for me.

I need to remember
that vision, the Light
that reflected
warmth, Wisdom and the
expanse of presence in
Love, in God.

This benevolent Source
reminds me when I crumble
into doubt, guilt, submission;
when I allow others to
squeeze the breath from
my spirit; when I do
not feel the beauty inside
of me, that It is always
with me, never leaves me
— never leaves any of us.

It reminds me that no matter the baggage
I carry, the dynamic
or rut I stumble in
or issues that bond to me,
I am still LOVE, because
that is where I come from.
That IS where the feet
of my spirit dance; that
IS where the Holy Spirit
sings to me.

2/13/07

†††

Empathic Light
electrifies the soul
moves Love
like water through us all

†††

"It is okay if you change direction,
there is no one right road.
The only wrong turn you can take
is to deny My Love, My Will,
My Grace. When you are full
of doubt or worthlessness, that
is not My Voice. That is not
how I speak to My children."

(Awoke at 2:00am with this message coming to me.)

†††

No longer "when?", do I
ask, Lord, but, "where?".
I give You my body
as living altar
I give these hands
as source of touch
these eyes
to speak Light
in darkness

I give You my voice
to caress
as breath of peace

Godhead-vision-focused
in gratitude for freewill
I give You my
life as prayer

†††

In giving the "body as living altar"
"life as prayer"
— living as a channel
of Grace for the
Love of God —
one must be ready to
know no boundaries...
For this body, this life
will truly live no boundaries
Sometimes confused,
eventually assured and aware
emotion, thought, word,
sensation, movement,
stillness, time, illness
and term are not
always its own...
It knows, in union
there is no "own"
One must be ready to
understand misunderstood
to be naked in all others'
clothes
impregnated "heathen"
"heretic" to the theologian
"hopeless" to the healer
"threat" to the psychiatrist

"anomaly" to the Holy
"unexplainable" to the medical
One must be ready
to be in not being
to not be in being
One must be ready
to be all opposites
for one will live the
fusion of all opposites

Giving the "body as living altar"
"life as prayer"
is not about theology
not about politic
nor propositional law
It is a deep walk
with and in the midst
of God
where union
defies definition

†††

Calling
music
pulls
to sway
stirs
rhythms
soaked
in broken-
bent
harmony
misunderstood
as mistaken r
e
Evolution Curled h
unfolds g
draws desire i
H
checks its truth
in those Eyes
and decides

to carry
acCHORDing
notes below
that soothe
an altered-womb-
altar

e
Vibratory Concern s
sings its song i
to cushion those knees a
r their head
in affection that
births to give
understanding
where it drinks again
in the Liquid Sound
of Wisdom
and sways no more
though limbs
dance

to flow over
melody
of Love
poured
to linger aroma
of Natural
Beauty
Pure

Thank You, Lord, for this
moment of fluidity...

All my Love
from Above
through all
and back again

I Evolve to lose myself in Creation
to love and respect this closest neighbor, humbly

2/18/08

†††

Our destiny is that of
Supernatural
where we return to our
beginning of Supernatural

Our "time" is that of
Supernatural

If, in our "time," we
remain aware of this
Supernatural
then we are living our
destiny
Here, rather than "It is not
the destiny but the
journey," the destiny
becomes the journey;
the journey becomes
the destiny

Destiny is the beginning
the existence
the return

Journey is the beginning
        the existence
        the return
To remain aware of this with
        open hearts
is to embrace our calling
is to understand Agape Love
is to love God with mind, heart
        and soul
is to love God in other
        with mind, heart and soul
is to love God internal
        with mind, heart and soul
is to fulfill the commandment
        and live our destiny

8/2/08

†††

May we be channels for Your
        Grace to enter this realm
May we be bridges of peace

May we be vessels for Your Vision
        in thought, word, all
        put forth from our being

May our hearts be a place
        of rest for Jesus
        and may we reflect
        that Heart as we are raised
        out of self and into You

Rather than journey toward a destiny,
        may we understand what it
        means to <u>live the destiny</u>
        by remaining aware of our
        Supernatural beginning, existence,
        return, all along our journey

Allow me, Father —
    if words, voice, truly are
    a gift given me, as many
    have said — the ability
    to combine penetrating
    intuition sensitively with
    words of support, encouragement,
    truth and enlightenment.
    Help me to continue to be a
        gentle vehicle...

Raise me out of self
and into You
Raise us out of self
and into You
Help us to reach out
in ways that gently
and compassionately
seek to understand
and embrace each other

Help us to restore hearts
and heal this age of
exploitation, frustration,
aggression, alienation,
fragmentation and
abusive persuasion
...this age of judgment
abounding that allows
for progressive fermentation
of darkness and oppression
to create anesthetized
machines out of
discarded, dignity
disregarded humans

8/3/08

†††

Always remain open to,
and aware of, the Good in
your soul and your life
will never be less than whole...

It speaks ever so gently, softly,
because It doesn't want to interfere
or intrude on our free will.
Yet, we feel It. As our spiritual longing
and sensitivity heighten we feel It
more strongly, like a rush of water;
a surge of electricity that moves us
more deeply inward to bring us further
forward as we come closer to a steady
consistent flow from the Eye of understanding
that raises our will to join with that of
Godhead consciousness. That of unity with
a consciousness that lies latent in us all,
connects us to all created — natural, Supernatural —
where we truly become indistinguishable.
"I" dissolves into "we" into "our" into
"no one" into "none" where fluid
evaporates into sound that evaporates
into vibration felt, then discovered,
then not felt but known, where movement
then occurs in stillness and stillness
moves as all lie down in One
Beat of Heart.

†††

Creation Sees Empty Full

Creation sees emptiness and full together,
for it sees apparent emptiness
as the foundation of possibility, and possibility
realized is full of all that made
that possibility. And, realized possibility is empty —
open to more possibility,
different directions, other doors, options, reasons
beyond our knowing and uses
beyond our intentions...

Duality / Non-Duality
Both exist...
To strive for non-duality
is the same as striving
for perfection,
to be perfectly Holy —
free of all sin

Anytime we strive for perfection
we are not living in awareness...
for we cannot experience
the joy
the peace
just from the experience

And the mountain
only seems to get higher
and if we do reach atop
it seems not high enough

In striving for perfection
I have missed so many
moments
so many
smiles
so many
flowers
angels
and sand-boxes...

Inter-be
Every smile ripples
to create a smile
for another
yet when a tear sheds
and we deeply see
to receive
that we are
one with that one
or one with
those shed from
within
compassion empties the heart
to be full
and the joy
of understanding
creates the bridge
of communion

aware none are
untouchable...

†††

Father, help me to walk what
I say, to be what I pray.
Help me to come to You with
All of me, to remove any veil,
for I need no guard in Your
presence. It is not You who
threaten my existence, but
You who make it possible to be,
You who breathe life through me.
Help us to truly understand
The Holy Spirit, Its capacity for
intimacy. Help us to know Your
omnipresence in that breath no
matter how stressed, preoccupied,
tucked far away we may feel.
Please do not refrain from speaking
through us, nor dancing in us.
Amen

Illuminated manuscript of Kimberlyann DeAngelo's
"Father, help me"
by Samuel Zimmerman

www.ingramcontent.com/pod-product-compliance
Lightning Source LLC
LaVergne TN
LVHW050535100826
845148LV00002B/564